A New Path

IBBETSON STREET PRESS
25 School Street
Somerville MA 02143

www.ibbetsonpress.com

ISBN 978-1-365-92235-0

Photographs by Joseph A. Cohen: Bahia Cohen p.17, Beth Bahia Cohen p.40, Sonia Cohen p.50, David Cohen p.68, Andy Cohen p.69, Peter Maina p.77, Joe's bench p.83

Back cover photo by Kevin Cohen. Boris and Ida Eisenstadt (Boris and Ida Eisenstadt were Sonia Cohen's parents) p.18, Joe in foxhole in Anzio p.7, cover photo of Joe, his father Aaron, and his brother Ezra at Coney Island, and wartime photo of Joseph and Sonia Cohen p.46: all by unknown photographers

A few poems in this book have been previously published in the Bagel Bards anthology, Ibbetson Street magazine, and Constellations

Book design by S.R. Glines
text: ITC New Baskerville

Introduction

It is a great honor to be invited to write the introduction to the second book of poetry, A New Path, by Joe Cohen, a man whose energy fills me with awe and inspiration. Though he was officially my student for many years, he has always been my teacher as well. From Joe I have learned to be more accepting, more feisty, and more appreciative of classical music. At the age of 99, Joe is still going strong – as a vital force of nature, a humanitarian, a family man, a friend, a devoted lover of nature and the arts, and a poet. As a matter of fact, now – having lived almost a century – he is in the process of following "a new path." I am proud and grateful that our worlds have overlapped.

Joe's second book, like his first, has content, themes, and rhythms all his own. Very much a product of his own consciousness and personality, it is filled with delight in the details of creation, creation as it is intrinsic to the natural world and as it manifests in human productivity. For Joe, beauty is what makes the world go round, the blood of existence. For him, without beauty, life is bland and meaningless.

Fortunately for Joe and for the rest of us, Joe finds beauty everywhere he looks – in his son Andy's "House in the Sky" overlooking the Pacific, in his self-proclaimed bench on Huron Avenue in Cambridge, in his ever-present love of Sonia, the wife he lost after 71 years of marriage, in his adoration of his musically gifted daughter, Beth, his dear sons David and Andy, his grandchildren and all of his family, and always in the "feast of music" he surrounds himself with. As he writes of his years with Sonia – "Some yearn for the hush of silence, but we opt for music, music, music."

From the beginning of their relationship, Sonia was Joe's inspiration, through her sensual beauty, her talent as a composer and pianist, and her ties to the cultural world that Joe's childhood had denied him. Even in the trenches during World War II, thoughts of Sonia drove Joe to Elizabethan heights of creativity:

"So when I lie in my deep dug fox hole,
I ponder the beauty that life's soil yields.
There are roses so red, fragrant and pure,
but lovelier than Sonia there are none, l am sure."

Underlying Joe's sensitive portraits is a decision to preserve the vitality of the people he describes: his beloved mother, Bahia, with her astonishing Old Country sayings, his daughter Beth, renowned musician, master of obscure and wonderful instruments, his deaf brother Abe who led a rich but silent life, his apartment concierge whom he dubs "Peter the Great." Joe's portraits give each of these people literary substance, re-creating them so that his readers can develop personal relationships with them.

One of the most distinctive elements of Joe's poetry is his palpable delight in diversity. Part of his joy in being in Cambridge is the wonderful mix of ethnicities he is part of every time he goes "Riding Up – Riding Down" in the elevator in his building. "How wonderful," he proclaims, "to traverse the globe in this small and intimate chamber." He takes great pleasure in the variety of multicultural activities reflecting "the Far East, the Middle East, Africa and Asia that are, in his new home base, as common as soap operas on afternoon TV."

The pleasure Joe takes in world cultures is not new. Even during his upbringing in a Syrian Jewish, rather restrictive environment, he yearned for multiculturalism. After all, he broke boundaries by marrying his darling Sonia who was outside the ethnic fold. All his life, Joe has sought to enlarge his world through the art, music, dance, and food of other cultures.

In keeping with this, Joe has always been an ardent supporter of human rights. From his brave service during World War II – for which he recently received the French Legion of Honor medal for serving in France, making him a Chevalier (Knight) – to his successful battle in 1950 to integrate the Levittown community on Long Island, he has not only recognized, but vigorously defended, the right of every human being to be treated with dignity and respect. This kind of moral imperative demonstrates that Joe, far from being a dreamy-eyed poet, is a person with strong convictions, well-aware of evils in the world and determined to be a force against them.

In spite of all the pain Joe has suffered in 99 years, he remains an optimist. He manages to find poetic inspiration in his apartment lobby, on a park bench, and even in a visit to the hospital. While he is well aware of physical limitations, he manages to make light of them, even to marvel at the devices that help us cope with them. Who but Joe Cohen would write loving poems to his eyeglasses, his cane, and his walker?

Joe fights evil and pain, loss and grief, in the way he knows best: by involving himself with beauty, both by admiring it and creating it. His fascination and participation in the arts is his answer to the demons that plague this world. Whether he is observing natural wonders, memorializing those he has lost with beautiful words, listening to Haydn's string quartets, or musing on the inconveniences of aging with acerbic wit, Joe Cohen creates poems that stand as a fortress against death itself.

Susan Astor
February 20, 2017

Dedication by Leah Giles

I have had the pleasure of working with Joe on his poetry for the past year and a half. The title of Joe's first book is A Full Life. An alternate title for this second book could be A Fuller Life, because Joe has continued to write, and live, and do. The book is a wonderful mix of poems on those experiences, from childhood to retirement. But the poems are not all strictly autobiographical; Joe is a keen observer who sees the sublime in the ordinary. He muses on the backs of the audience's heads at a concert, the power of photography, and the vibrance of Cambridge.

Joe's poetry resonates because it speaks to our common thoughts and experiences; we can see ourselves, or others we know, in the poems about change, aging, family. Joe's lines are lyrical but not cryptic; they are relatable and understandable, and they are often humorous. But the poems also challenge us to see things in new ways. Everything from a stormy harbor scene to a doctor's waiting room to a park bench come alive through Joe's words. He has a deep belief in the power of the human spirit and our capacity to constantly discover.

Joe has taught me more than he knows. I am amazed by his creativity and passion; his dedication to trying new things–well into his ninth decade; his experiences of love and war, of family and music and so much more. Thank you, Joe, for your friendship and encouragement. May your poems continue to inspire others as you have inspired me.

Acknowledgements

My deepest thanks to my daughter Beth for her unwavering encouragement, support and work to help create this book.

I am profoundly grateful to my mentor and poet friend Susan Astor for her editing, expertise, and generous and thoughtful introduction.

My warmest thanks to Leah Giles who worked with me on this book for 1 ½ years.

Without her help, I could not have done it.

Contents

A New Path

selected poetry

of

Joseph A. Cohen

New World Or Old?

My parents, sailing westward from Syria,
landed where old neighbors
had previously settled.
A first generation son of immigrants,
I plunged into America's freewheeling ways
with confusion.

No dust on empty bookshelves,
no toys to clutter precious living space,
yet we flourished in our insulated society.
We breathed in the vigor of the new land
while clinging to the mores of Aleppo.

On my block, I knew many but spoke to few.
Relatives and the newly arrived filled our days.
What need had we for others?
The hum of a day's rhythm reflected
eating, drinking, happy but noisy talk.

Punch ball, stick ball, "Johnny on a pony 1 2 3"
helped us to meld into the West.
Neighbors not so newly arrived
showed occasional hostility
towards our crowded households.

There came a time when new and old cultures clashed.
Did I have to choose to commit to only one?
Naive and innocent, I stumbled on the answer:
Why not enjoy the treasures of both?

To See Or Not

It was like the change
from night to day.
At the age of eight,
the miracle of seeing better
surprised and thrilled me.
Faces were easier to recognize,
scenery was more colorful,
and all the world so much more focused.

The glasses fit snugly like blinders on a horse.
I was different from the kids
who laughed at me and called me
four-eyes. It hurt to be teased.

But now in class I could see numbers
on the blackboard.
I could recognize
faces, forms, as never before.
I became part of the scene.
I even smacked a homerun playing stickball
by walloping a rubber ball with a broom stick.

My first pair of glasses
became one with me. I read more
than ever without suffering headaches.

Life became fuller, richer
and more accessible.
I was proud of my four eyes
that helped me to be involved with
the world about me.

My First Voyage

I remember when I first set sail.
It was raining and the icy wind
tore through my clothes.
Bleak was the mood, a frigid
gray cast hung over the scene.

Ships that sail in the dawn
moved out of port while
anti-aircraft balloons swayed in the wind.
Escort planes circled protectively while
a grim fleet of destroyers tended
to this convoy of fifty troop ships.

Wonderment and fear of the unknown
gave way to "hitting the rail" as we gave
back our breakfasts. We ploughed
through rough waters in the open seas
as I sat back to suffer a journey
of eighteen seasick days to Casablanca,
thus beginning my three-year stint overseas
fighting the "good war" - World War II.

On Looking At Sonia's Portrait

With a touch of inspiration from an Elizabethan poet

And whilst I look upon your face,
I dream of nights full of your embrace.
Your brave and wistful, yearning expression
shows much of love's sincerest passion.

So when I lie in my deeply dug foxhole,
I ponder the beauty that life's soil yields.
There are roses so red, fragrant and pure,
but lovelier than Sonia there are none, l am sure.

On guard at night when war doth sleep,
to the strains of a symphony my heart doth leap.
Amidst the star-roofed quiet countryside,
my mind reflects on my musical bride.

How oft when thou great music play,
my soul to the rhythm of your fingers sway.
And now your tender eyes to me impart
your melodious love though we're far apart.

(Written during my WWII army stint overseas)

Giuseppe

With the invasion of Anzio imminent,
all leaves were cancelled. A performance
of *Tosca* at the local opera house went on
without my eager presence.

I was engaged in waterproofing our anti-aircraft
cannons when he strolled by cranking out
O Sole Mio on his fiddle. I asked if he
played *musica classica.* With
pride he replied, "Si, signore." How grand it
was for me to have a private concert while
serving overseas.

Dismissing my gun crewmates, I volunteered
to finish invasion preparations alone while enjoying
music by Beethoven, Mozart, and Bach
played by an Italian street musician.

Amid the roar of planes giving us cover,
while swarms of small crafts loaded, churning
the waters of the port of Salerno, he lifted
his bow above the violin and waited for one full minute
before playing Bach's concerto for violin #1.

Hours later he was wrung dry from playing
beautiful music in an atmosphere far from
the quiet dignity of a concert hall.
I rewarded
him in the only way I knew how, by drowning
him with candy, smokes and army issue towels.

Before midnight, the 451st AAA battalion
boarded an LST and steamed up the Italian
coastline in the glare of a full moon to land
behind Nazi lines at Anzio.

Love Story

Amidst the war's destruction, they met.
He, a soldier, she, a PhD candidate at Rome University.
Lying wounded in an army hospital
in Naples, it was Gabriella who nurtured him.

To be closer to Jimmy, she became
an American Red Cross hostess.
Love's pace quickens at such times,
and their passion deepened in an atmosphere
of coffee, doughnuts and V-mail writing desks.

At a soirée for some of us
soon to go on another invasion,
she served dainty sandwiches.
When asked why the beef was so
sweet, she said it was horse meat.

Before I left, she asked me if she would
be happy in America accepting
his fervent proposal of marriage.
How could I play God with lives
of young lovers in wartime?

I learned later that she would not
leave her family and the land of her birth.
He became despondent over her rejection
and never achieved his potential
as a fine artist on his return home.

Larry The Lover

A fruit handler from Brooklyn,
a skinny, simple lad in uniform,
demanding very little from life.

World War II found us in a quiet
village of Loncin, Belgium.
For most of us, exposure to war dangers
usually lasted only a few minutes a day.

Days passed monotonously,
leaving much time to seek
romance away from home.

Pretty Deidre who lived near
our gun position was the subject
of fantasies enjoyed and relived
by men of section five.

She took a fancy to Larry although
he spoke no French and she, no English.
Translation became my job as one
who spoke both languages.

They communicated through gestures,
eye movements, and body language.
Amidst exploding V1 robot missiles
they courted with touching innocence.

One day on an open deck coming home,
the machos swaggered up to him
and asked about Diedre.
When told about this torrid love affair,
they raged and grabbed him by his neck.
That this runt was a lover of the *Rose
of Loncin* was unbelievable!

Only when I was asked to tell
of this tender, lonely, and passionate
wartime affair of the heart
did they believe him. I may have saved
him from being thrown overboard.

Levittown Was White

A stretch of potato farms on Long Island
was transformed into a low-cost housing
development for returning WWII veterans.

I moved my small family in and then discovered
that the owner, William Levitt,
refused to rent or sell to anyone who wasn't Caucasian.

Together with my African American friend Bill Cotter,
we formed the Committee to End Discrimination
in Levittown.
Leaflets were distributed,
residents were canvassed to gather support,
civil rights groups, local press,
notables like Eleanor Roosevelt and
Phillip Murray were alerted
and their messages of support
were read at a large planning meeting.

On Christmas Eve 1950, a truck carrying the
household belongings of Mr. and Mrs. Leroy Cannon
pulled up to a house
on a quiet street in Levittown.
The parade of good people carrying things
from the truck started and after several hours,
the first family of color now was living
in a formerly all-white community.

We reveled through the night,
hoping that rumblings from local KKK elements
would die down, as we celebrated
the principles of brotherhood, equality and
the biblical commandment "Love thy Neighbor."

To insure the safety of the Cannon family,
the Committee arranged to have two men
sleep in the attic of a sympathetic neighbor
every night for four months.
Despite our success in 1950, today there are only
a small number of black families
living in Levittown.
The struggle still has a long way to go.

My Mother Bahia

Having emigrated to America from Syria in 1911,
she spoke little English.
She mothered her eight children in Arabic.

If I asked for money for a second ice cream cone, she replied
in her native language, "chaud lahmeh." (tear my flesh)
When playing stickball I often batted a ball
through a neighbor's window.
As cops appeared to investigate, she berated them
and hugged me, saying "ibnee mneeh, roohu howeshu il buam."
(My boy, good boy, leave him alone, go chase crooks)

She woke us, washed us, fed us, and sent the clan to school
after which she cleaned the house and left
to visit friends and play cards.
At night after lights went out,
we could read only with flashlights under blankets.

When once I asked her to buy a used piano, she refused,
suggesting that I go to my room and think about business.

Each night at dinner, my father filled a vinegar cruet with scotch
whiskey only to have her pour half of it back into the bottle.
She ran the household like a drill sergeant.

She drove the family car slowly,
complaining that other drivers on the road were speeding.
She sang Arabic songs while at the wheel.
Although she was illiterate,
she got her driver's license by bribing the inspector.
She opposed my marriage to a non-Syrian woman
who was a beautiful and talented pianist.
Making a surprise visit one day, she found me on the floor
scrubbing the kitchen linoleum.
She cried, "ish ha shida? Mautee!" (What is this? I should die!)

Boris The Gentle

Newly arrived from Belarus in 1922,
after stealthily crossing borders and an ocean,
he settled with his family in New York.
This new world was strange but free,
bewildering but safe.

With sparkling eyes he watched
over his four daughters.
In addition to running his homey
grocery store, he provided comfort
and warmth to his family.

Nothing caused him to lose patience.
Beloved by his customers,
he cheerfully wrapped slabs of butter,
filled cartons with sour pickles,
bagged fresh seeded rolls.

For decades he helped his wife Ida
rear four feisty girls,
always giving each love and hope.
Ravaged by overwork and an
ailing heart, he passed away too soon.

Never, never will the Eisenstadt daughters
cease to adore Boris the Gentle.

My Muse

She helps me write
a likely phrase, a playful word,
lines that flow with ease.
She guides an eager hand as
musical word pictures unravel.

Autumn colors mirror the mood,
red, orange, with bright gold splashes.
Winds whip through trees
as if to hasten the baring of branches.

A poem appears
with the flood of words
while gusts of ideas funnel
into graceful stanzas.

I bow in awe before the magic force
that fires restless fingers.

The Portrait

"Hold still," I cautioned as I composed the shot,
hoping the image I saw would print
with the same warmth and charm.
I tried to capture the look, the shape,
the balance and the inner self of the sitter.

Never will it change or move.
The expression pictured will freeze for all time.
Sometimes framed, it will hang quietly forever
never to respond to life around it.

It will look down on continuing existence
with rigid stillness and seeming indifference
unaffected by emotion or love.
It was created to mirror a mood,
a moment in history.

Trio

Handwoven of textured silk,
the tapestry hangs above
an ebony grand piano.
Its greens and grays
grace its share of the room.

Within a shadow's length,
a brooding bronze figure of a woman
sculpted by Puccinelli
cringes with pain.

As if to claim seniority,
an antique Chinese vase
reflects its glow from a
cracked porcelain surface.

With calm and quiet,
all three,
fabric, bronze, and porcelain,
live on together, eloquent in their silence.

Tennis In The Morning

Watching a player clad in tennis shorts
striding to the courts is to see
a committed person.
There is bustle around the board
where park cards are hung.
A hum of idle chatter hangs over
the waiting area while partners
seek each other or try to get a third or fourth.

Greetings are exchanged
as warm up exercises begin.
Arms, legs, torsos
flung up, down around.

Sunblock flows in torrents
like Snake River downstream rapids.
Despite the buzz of agitation
while waiting for gates to open,
an overall serenity prevails.
As kids, we worried if anyone had a ball.
Were there enough players to form two sides?
Could we find an empty lot to play on?

Now we know where we play,
we have titanium rackets,
foursomes are arranged in advance,
courts are watered, neatly brushed.
Let our obsession begin.

My Window

I see through my window
the quiet of a sleepy afternoon

A bumblebee buzzing
spanning four window panes

The silence within, the hum without,
another summer day

The Beckoning

As winter is eased out
by spring showers and warm sunshine,
bare branches await new foliage.

Soon gentle hills with
greenery, lush and lively,
will be nourished by
heavenly melodies.

This, Tanglewood, mecca to
lovers of music crowding shed and halls eagerly.
Spreading over luxuriant lawns
with gourmet picnic baskets,
they toast Saint Cecilia, patron saint of music.

Strolling through the grounds,
one hears strains of a symphony to the left,
a string quartet from the right,
and down below, a student singing a lied.

Day and night, notes high and low,
charge the grass, resonate from Elysian fields.
Woodwinds vie with strings and brass
to charm the senses and captivate the mind.

Sound the trumpets,
listen to bird-like flutes,
swoon to sweet violins and vibrant cellos.
Tramp to powerful tympani,
marvel at harmonious voices
blending with nature's own songs.

My Desk

It is not of rolltop vintage
that hides chaos.
It is rather flat with yards
of space on which to pile papers.

Rarely does its white oak grain
appear from under mountains
of items strewn in studied disorder.
It would appear that storage
is its primary function.

Documents are moved endlessly
yet they never disappear.
To find one is like
digging for mountain gold.

When oh when will I find
a long-lost bill, precious notes or
a much-needed phone number?

I say never! So I may as well relax
and enjoy the life of a desk slob.

We Flew

Lightning, shattering turbulence
rocked us as the flying machine groped
to stay in the murky air lane.
Could we recover from the next dip?
Would the shocks of being slammed
left, right, upwards, and downwards
give victory to the Angel of Death?
Flying on the big bird was much
like breaking in a wild bronco.
The roar of the engines, usually even, sputtered,
coughed in a troubled mode.
We had no thoughts of food or drink
while our lives seemed
to hang on a single thread.
After what seemed to be
a lifetime of terror, the pilot
announced with a casual drawl that
New York was only 100 miles to the south.
In a flash, we broke through the clouds.
Within minutes, we landed softly like
a feather on a balloon.

We

I am of medium height, you are short.
I bellow, you speak softly.
I awake with gusto, you reel from sleep.
I stride with no restraint, you step gracefully.
My family is large, yours is tiny.
I barbeque pompously with a flourish,
you cook masterfully and
season food like a French chef.
You remember birthdays, I mutter, "again?"
You prefer a fastidious house, I could live in chaos.
But we both know
that opposites sometimes attract.

Life In My Garden

How like a miniature world
is my garden retreat,
bounded by stately trees,
once meek and spindly.

A pastoral symphony
sounds the music of trees,
leaves, birds
singing to a background
of buzzing, clacking insects.

A lone metal sculpture
stands like a sentry on a sloping green lawn,
with squirrels darting up trees and down.

One is never alone in my garden.

A Day At The Met

It is sunny in the park this day —
a park that winds around the Metropolitan
Museum of Art with loving embrace.
Folks walk, chat, drink in the beauty
of trees and rolling hills
lined with winding paths.

Standing in front of the museum building,
we are in the shadow of Greek columns
on each side of welcoming doors.
The buzz of lovers of art fills the lobby
as they go from gift shops to imposing exhibits.

It is unbelievable that *where 'ere you walk,*
great paintings, magnificent statuary and
unforgettable artifacts surround you.

Harking back to ancient times
opens the mind to another world, a world
so different, so strange.
We luxuriate for the moment
as we imagine living in Rome or
Greece with the proud heroes
and heroines of another day.

Awakening

Dancing images paint the wall with wind
and sun playing the shadow symphony.
Morning vigor stirs the branches fueled
by a yellow, foggy sunrise.
Gusts of air conduct the wavy wisps of leaf-filled boughs.
Nuances of nature draw bold lines and circles
across the entire canvas.
Passing clouds soften the shadows
to the moaning of the matin's dirge.
Soon the sun emerges to
brighten the flickering choreography.
In a flash I awake to a new day
soon to be crowded with mundane
chores and sounds of daytime living.

The Recital

A young pianist glides to the piano.
With a quivering calm, she adjusts
the bench, pauses, and, with studied concentration,
plays the opening notes.

Shortly, she is fully immersed
in the performance. Melodies
and chords formed with both hands
are woven to sound the glorious music.

Gentle themes sing out in the
second movement, filling the
concert hall with ineffable beauty.
She reflects the composer's surge
with crescendos and rapid runs.

Playing with discipline, with intense concentration,
she recreates the music as if she composed it.

Nature's Greenhouse

Pink and blue tulips stand tall,
graceful, giving color to the green canvas.
Proud, stately, they cup their petals
to herald the warmth and beauty of spring.

How like a rose to inspire bards
to sing of its beauty.
Braided garlands adorn brows of brides
Rose petals are strewn underneath
footsteps along lovers paths.

Dogwoods lie still
yet always
seem to be dancing
to the rhythm of the wind.
Blooming early, they are
harbingers of the new, the young,
of nature's flowering.

Timid crocuses periscope up through
thawing earth with disbelief
at the new seasons warmth. It is true
that the snow and ice cover
will not last forever?

Crawling, climbing, twisting,
ivy covers tradition
soaked walls of learning.
Unwanted, it creeps nonetheless
meaning to stay as the cover of yesteryear.

The Songs Of Angels

Brandenburg concertos
performed *tutti* or solo,
played *con affetuoso*
with movements *adagio* and *presto*.
Whether in the cadenza or trio,
our joy teeming *con brio*.
Give thanks for this overflow
of tunes and arias bel canto.

To enjoy this festive season
we bless good health for sound reason.
A mug of beer to toast
this time of cheer with song.
Oratorios with arias sublime,
vibratos and trills quiver from strings.
Let us ring through the concert halls
And sound melodious calls for
"peace and goodwill to all."

Hawanim, Playing And Singing
on The Banks of the Nile

From points far west of Cairo,
they gather for a joyous rehearsal.
Instruments are unsheathed – a violin,
an *oud*, a *kanoun (zither)*, a set of frame drums (*bendirs*).

All are women, women enamored of
the music of the Middle East.
They feast on Nicole's gourmet spread
before rich melodies fill the room.
Beth, the hostess, pours wine lavishly.

Calmed and soothed
by Syrian food and drink,
the tuning begins.
Anne Elise sits formally to tune
her 64 stringed *kanoun*,
Marina cuddles her rounded *oud*
and plucks double strings with a turkey feather
to adjust the pitch.
Nicole lays out her *bendir* and *derbeka*
while Beth tunes her violin.
Sarra, a young Sudanese singer,
warms up her earthy voice.

A first in America perhaps,
the women band together
to perform classical Arabic music.

In contrast to olden days,
they perform in public,
a feat rarely seen in the old country,
where women only belly-danced
and sang for sheiks and pashas.

Intimate Music

From the last row, I see
gray heads and bald ones
sway from side to side.

Who will replace these
children of the depression
when bells sound for them?

For some of our first generation youth,
chamber music was new, exciting and way out.
To discover another of Beethoven's late quartets
was to strike gold forever.

This genre became a religious happening
crowned with jewels by
Mozart, Brahms and Schubert.
The fortunate studied music
and played duets, trios, and quartets.
Cellists were sought after
with bribes of gourmet dinners.

Due to the thinning of the ranks,
Alice Tully Hall, temple of
chamber music, is no longer
a meeting place for the old gang.
Strangers new to the rolls
fill the seats, but will they
renew subscriptions for
twenty-five years running?

Would that the new ones,
black-haired and blonde, become the
guardians of "Musique de Chambre!"

Malibu By The Sea

Early of a morning,
sunrise sprays the ocean,
sending reflections to dance
across blue waters.

Air warms to the rising sun,
gulls glide and surfers swerve.
Waves pound the shore
with relentless crashes,
breaking nature's silence.

Towards evening, the sun dips into
darkening waters, casting
fiery red light on sky,
clouds, and all the world.
Fresh sweet winds blow
to greet the cover of night.
Music from the ocean's rumbling is soft,
constant and soothing.

My Friend Irving Weissman

It was a fine man we came to honor.
Eighty plus years he struggled
for a better life for all and always
he lived to the full.

Friends spoke of his humanity and what
he gave to the world around him.
They recalled his feistiness and humor as
he beamed warmth to all he met.

There was Irving, writer, historian, the soldier who
battled fascism twice,
once in Spain and again in World War II.

Irving, who was always curious about life.
As his sun was setting,
he spoke to nurses about politics,
James Joyce and history,
but never about sports.

Always in charge of his own life,
he asked his nurse if the oxygen tank
kept him alive and when she said that
it helped, he indicated it was now time for him to die.

Before he left us, he cried out to his daughter Ann,
"What a fascinating world we live in."

The Return

We welcome Beth from journeys to the lands
of Homer and Mustafa Kemal.
Warmth and love sweep through the door
as she floats in with instruments,
bundles and waves of joy. With wine to
celebrate, we listen to tales of
Mediterranean nights.

Boating in the Bosphorus, island-hopping
in Greece, friendships borne of music,
being welcomed into Turkish households-
this is the fruit of living in Anatolia
and on a mountain top on the Greek island of Andros.

Playing nine bowed instruments and
delving into the musical modes of
taxims and traditional village dances,
she is preserving endangered treasures
from the onslaught of electronic, rock,
and popular music which
spreads like a black cloud.

None but a few enjoy their life's work.
For her to have mastered the Greek *violi*, the
Turkish *yayli tanbur* is to realize many of the
goals and hopes of an artist.
Never a night without a feast of music.

A New Path

Loss of youth
need not be so tragic.
The pace of life's pleasures can slow down
gracefully and gently.

The tempo need not be as lively as it was
to continue to yield satisfaction, joy, fulfillment.
Love of music, art, fine literature,
the visual creations does not
demand muscles or speed.

Though slashing forehand drives in tennis
are a dream from the past,
other advantages warm the color of life today.
New wisdom drawn from living longer
enriches the ability to deal with people
and problems of aging.

The music of Brahms is just as fulfilling.
Mona Lisa's mysterious expression
remains as intriguing as it did
when we were young.

To grow anew with freshness is
to respond to new challenges.
It is time to awaken latent talents
and move to enrich the quality of life.

How many letters to write, notes to read,
books to dig into?
How many hobbies to develop
that have waited for years?

Though we are no longer vigorous and powerful,
it is time to stop the moaning,
to cease the whining, to go forth
to drink in the pleasures of creativity and exploration.

My Brother Abe - A Tribute

Born deaf, from the time he went to school at Fanwood
to his life on the beaches at Margate,
Abe smiled warmly.
He worked with me at Sunweave Linen for many years.
Often, the staff spoke to him eagerly
since he taught them to sign during lunch breaks.
Humor was key in discussions.
So many became friends although
it was mainly women who were most sensitive
and eager to learn a new language.

Father of two children himself, his ability
to communicate has always been magical.
At family gatherings he was often surrounded
by young ones to joke and gossip in sign language.

Ever since childhood he was a beach person
so the move to Florida was fitting.
He did not need a suntan for his
good looks to radiate sunshine.
He did not play handball in recent years
but he swam and splashed
like a teenager till the end.

His lovely wife Marcia brought him profound
and lasting happiness.
Bright, intellectual and keenly aware,
she helped to make their life a joy.
They migrated with their deaf community
to a small town in Florida to live
a rich but silent life till the end.

In sign language, "I bid you
good-bye, Abe. We will miss you."

We Used To Drive

We drove to work, to play, to meet with friends.
We drove to eat, to vacation, to fill our lives
with pleasure.

When we no longer grab the wheel to go and come,
our lives take on a different pace. When the urge to
head for destinations cannot be satisfied,
feverish frustration sets in.

How will we go? Who will drive us?
It was easier before.
It was more natural to be in motion at will.
Shorn of car and ignition key,
we ask ourselves not when, but how.
Now we are dependent on cabs,
private drivers and friends.

As we age, our buddies begin to dwindle.
Some pass on, others go south
and still others cannot drive anymore
or limit their driving to daylight.

It is not the worst but it is not the best. We adapt to new
technologies.
We are deluged by computers, email, cell phones, iPads.
We learn to develop hobbies and art forms
that we can engage in at home.
We depend on having needed supplies delivered.
There are ways to cope.
But oh! what a gift from heaven it would be to
open the car door
slide in and start her up.

Das Lied

If music be the food of love,
we feasted on Bach's French Suites.
We courted on the velvet-covered
pews at the musical services of the
First Presbyterian Church on Fifth Ave.
while listening to the great masses and passions.
"Our Song" was Beethoven's string quartet op.132.

Oh to live and love at such a time.
After hearing Beethoven's first symphony,
we danced at the prospect of capturing
the heart and soul of eight more, especially
the Ode To Joy, the climax of the Ninth.

For over 70 years we rejoiced
by listening to chamber music one evening, lieder
the next, and opera the following.
I wonder if a relationship can flourish by feeding on
one theme.
We find it safe to say: yes it can.

The House In The Sky

The white house on the hill
overlooking the grand Pacific
stands high and gracious,
looking down on all below.
It alone is the star.
Absorbing the warmth of the
sun and the moon's white glow,
it drinks in the lively sounds of the earth.
This beacon-like abode on high
shrugs off whipping winds and
driving rains.
It protects from the damp coldness
while giving shelter.
Like a lonely lighthouse,
it surveys all within its sight.
It provides warmth to those living
within its walls.
Lights from sturdy windows are visible
from far, far away.
From its perch well above the endless waters,
the silent building stands proudly and boldly,
sheltering my son and my three grandchildren.

Yearning

When will it end, the cold, the chill,
jailing us indoors for months?
When will the bright sun warm
the soft breezes caressing
our fragile bones?

Each morning we seek
a message promising that winter will
give way to a new life blessed by
lovely flowers in bloom, trees dressed in
fresh green leaves rustling in shy breezes.

Our spirits hang on light, on warmth,
on nature's awakening once again
as it has since it all began. True,
winter's darkness invites reading,
writing and quiet time to meditate.

But after a cold gloomy season
monotonously the same,
we cry out, *when will it end?*

Lovely Sonia

You remind me of gentle
warm breezes of a summer's day.
You remind me of the last note of
a Beethoven sonata.
When I am alone, I am reminded of
how you look upon awakening-
so tender, so thrilling.
At night just before my eyes are
yielding to sleep, you remind me of a pianist
swaying while playing a Mozart Sonata.
By day you remind me of gentle lapping of
lake waters at the shore line.
Truly I love
to be reminded of your smile, glance
and sparkling eyes as you respond to a
compliment to your beauty.

The Frick

Great art lives on while
the good folks pass in
and fade out.

We were young, eager
to drink in the joy of looking
at paintings and sculptures, works
that are sure to be there, always.
Politics, wars, health problems
drench our lives but
the Frick Collection still looks
down at us with grace and dignity.

Revisiting the scene
of our early courtship, ignoring
that I walk with a cane, that Sonia
sits proudly in her wheelchair,
we know that the art we came to see
will be there to see and enjoy.

Central Park, the Frick Mansion
graced by the majesty of Fifth Ave -
everything is still in place as it was
sixty-eight years ago.

Back then, on many a Sunday afternoon after
a stroll in the park, we would enter
the hallowed guardian of precious treasures
to thrill to the genius of Hals, Rembrandt,
Goya, among others.

We would wander through the Oval room,
the West gallery, resting in
the garden court on marble benches
while gazing upon the gentle fountain.

Moving softly on the silent floors
between the elegant columns, we relived
our early romantic trysts. We rekindled
our passions which fired up
as we looked upon paintings we now
consider our personal friends.

My Cane

Old men wave wooden canes
at kids who tease them.
Mine serves as my third leg.
It supports my aging frame,
levels my balance as I weave,
bend and step up and down.

While navigating outdoors
I grip a well-worn handle
as the steady tap
heralds my every move.

There are times when I brandish it,
twirl it or lean on it for full support.
Mine is inlaid with a pleasant design
so different from common wood ones.
Worn at the grip and rubber tip
it has creaked for many years.

Despite my gripes, were I to lose it
I would sorely miss it. In fact I
have even grown to like and depend
on my trusty rod.

The Long Wait

It seems to be the eternal wait.
Sitting in a crowded waiting room
we wait out our turn to see our doctor.
Our minds wander as we seek to
remember what we came for.
Our aches, pains, our new concerns,
all to be mentioned.

It is not a time to relax or to reflect
on pleasures we used to enjoy.
Are we getting old, slowing down?
Do we need more attention and have
less time to do what we want to?

There are things I worry about.
Did I wear underwear without a tear?
Did I shower well?
To endure this torture
I finger worn and torn magazines
having no interest for me.
Titles like *Horse and Hound, Food and Wine,*
Motor Trend, Woman's World
do not grip my attention.

From time to time a nurse calls out names
but mine seems to be a medical secret.
Patients exit the inner black cave of mystery,
sometimes relieved, sometimes bewildered.

My main fear is a serious illness.
Will I be able to live the life I have chosen?
As we age, the waits seem longer
as we ponder what
the good doctor will say.

I Remember

I remember being young enough to leap
up two steps at a time.
I also recall when my youth
permitted me to run long enough to get
my second wind.
There was a time when
we even played touch-tackle four hours at a
stretch on cold winter days.

It is hard to forget the happy hours I spent
going to concerts of the Budapest String Quartet
with my buddies, winding up having coffee at the Automat.
Joyful it is to visualize seeing and hearing
my intended as part of a piano duet playing
Brahms Hungarian Dances.

Unforgettable were the interests developed
by our children –
Andy into cars, David playing
drums with a jazz combo, Beth practicing her
music on her treasured violin.

Vivid and lengthy was my army service overseas
in the "Good War."
Bombs exploded much too close.
Seared in my memory are the more than 1,000
letters that I wrote daily to Sonia from foxholes.

Proudly, I recall a leading role I played in helping
to desegregate Levittown, NY.

I find it hardest to put out of my mind
the night my beautiful Sonia
was broken by a massive stroke
after attending an opera at the Met.

Music For Living

Music for us has been an elixir of joy,
sweetening hours of each day,
softening the pain, the loneliness.

When she was released after a short
hospital stay, her aide joined us
in singing Beethoven's Ode To Joy -
Marina in Georgian, Sonia in Russian
and I in Arabic.

It is wondrously healing
for a recovering artist-musician
to hear Bach cantatas back to back.

Upon awakening each morning, a Brahms trio
sets the stage for a long day of therapy,
good eating, reading,
and playing piano duets with Marina.

Dining graciously to Mozart's *Cosi Fon Tutti*
adds delicious taste and zest to the meal.

Slipping into bed to soaring melodies
of Haydn's Emperor String Quartet soothes
pressures from the day's activities.

Some yearn for the hush of silence,
but we opt for music, music, music.

Poignant Pauses

As violinists raise bows
awaiting the conductor's upbeat

Precious minutes after lights go out
before slipping off to sleep

Just before the first shovel of earth
falls on the coffin

Lying in a foxhole at night
awaiting another shelling barrage

After reading a new poem
to classmates while waiting
for ooh's, ah's, or just silence

Waking from a bad dream
realizing it was only a dream

Finishing a good book
moving to close it fondly

When the curtain falls
before the burst of applause

A passionate flash preceding a farewell kiss
placed on a beloved's lips

Life With A Walker

Strong, sleek and solid, it awaits my clutch.
Decked in black and white, it is poised to barge forward.
It keeps me active on two restless feet eager to leap.
Holding handlebars so firmly, I cannot wait to fly.
I can run, race or just keep up the pace.
No longer do I feel like an immovable fire hydrant.
When a pause is called for, I am able
to sit on the seat with comfort and ease.
Do I miss my lost balance or the surge up and down?
Maybe I do, but what a treasure sits at my side
when I am called upon to move onward.

Sonia's Angels

Deep in Sonia's life they weave
their magic: Arline an artist, Pat
a musician.
With tender concern
they give her a will to live - to live creatively.

With art and music lessons
these two precious beings help
to lift Sonia from the limitations
of a massive stroke.

Art on Mondays, music on Wednesdays,
days most sacred to her. With religious
fervor she paints and practices to be
ready for the next lessons.

Like clockwork, each appears
with a bag of gifts, one with
paintbrushes, the other with
new music to be studied.

She celebrates a life
of four score and five this year -
she blesses these charming women
with giving hearts.

Natela From Georgia

Flying in from a former Soviet republic,
she absorbs a new culture in a breeze.
The way we speak, the way we think
is ever so different from back home.
Fear of government and police is not universal here.

No different from tourists in Tbilisi, she eagerly takes in
museums, concerts and operas in New York.
Sunday mornings in Penn station,
women companions from Georgia gather to plan their day off.
Looking to her as their cultural leader,
they follow her to see and do things in New York
or they visit Brighton Beach, "Little Russia."
News, gossip, tips on what to find where
she gets from local Russian language newspapers and radio.

Although born in a mountain village,
her years in Tbilisi, the capital,
molded her intellect.
Having lived during the Communist era
which was followed by a shattered economy,
she left her homeland to find work in America
as a companion to support her extended family.

For us, she is a jewel from the Caucasus.

Where But Here

One fine day in spring, I came upon the essence of the land I live in.
It was an ordinary day in the life of a nonagenarian
seeking medical care at the North Shore LIJ Hospital at Manhasset.

Since I no longer drive, we use cabs.
The sleek limo was driven by Benita, a lively woman from Peru.
In the emergency room Sonia was attended to by Dr. Salvador,
a gentle female physician from El Salvador.
The long wait, the sweat, the tension were not eased
by the head medical man who nervously fended off
questions dealing with admission or dismissal.
Interestingly, he was one of the only non-immigrants we dealt with.

A thrilling sequence to the long procedure was a visit from Dr. Kendal,
a surgeon from Nepal, who with a a happy smile announced that Sonia
was not a candidate for surgery.
Alfonse, the lad who navigated the gurney to our room was from Haiti.
He and I sang a Creole lullaby
riding through the long halls at midnight.

Within minutes, Maria, the night nurse from the Philippines, took
charge and put my wife to bed. I was to spend the night in a chair
next to Sonia's bed counting the seconds till morning.
At about 2 A.M. a tall African American nurse, Joan Coburn, glided
in to check pulse, fever, blood pressure.

Early the next morning the hospital came alive
with the buzz of caregivers tending to their patients.
Our angel, day nurse Shoba from Trinidad, entered as if
on wings of song to attend to my darling wife.

That evening, Sonia's roommate was visited by her large Sicilian family.
Although the mood was somber it soon came alive.
Beth, our daughter, had her violin with her and they asked
for some music. Soon a party atmosphere fell over the whole room.

She played Italian folk songs.
They all sang, laughed and cheered up for the
brief moments of the party –
a welcome relief from hospital gloom.

For about 24 hours, we were involved
with a host of new and old Americans
all living and working under a banner:
"All-American."

Was A Time

Was a time when we bitched, griped,
swore to pass the day away as G.I.s.
We rode in a 6x6 army truck, swerving
and roaring up and down
Italian hill-town roads
whistling at young peasant girls.

Now six decades later, we
ride a 4x4 van to a V.A. medical center,
still casualties of WWll.
Silent, pensive, self-absorbed, we endure the
twists, turns and bumps of the two-hour ride.

Baseball caps draped over gray hair
replace woolen beanies; the drab jackets
match the lifeless mood. Men with pale faces,
some reflecting pain, some early morning
stupor, fill the seats of the van transporting us.

Entering the doors of a modern building
with hallways sunshine-lit, we
are greeted by a bevy of loving angels.
From receptionists to physicians,
all smile, listen, offering to help in any which way.
Moving from clinic to clinic, our health needs
are addressed with the fruits of modern medicine.

As we pile into the van for the return home,
I look out at the center with fondness and respect.

Obviously, from top leadership down, this V.A. team
has not forgotten that "we served."

Why It Was So Good

I never could imagine a stay
in a hospital could be good.
A recent one fooled me -
it proved to be memorable.

Being a full-time caregiver for my wife
after her massive stroke, suddenly I was the
one being cared for.

At 7:30 A.M. a radio droned on about
a weather reading of one degree outside.
After being awakened for pills, checking
of vitals and even having blood drawn,
I realized that I only had to wait for
food and more medical tests.

Rest without pressures aroused
the desire to move, work and even
to be creative.

Time had not always been plentiful
but now it enveloped me.
Time to plan, time to reflect,
time to fit it all into my life's pace.

To finish the *Sunday Times*,
to read two books simultaneously,
to take a catnap
with no chores waiting to be finished,
to write several poems,
to edit again and again -
that is why it was so good.

Our Home In Great Neck

The time has arrived for us to leave our warm comforting home
to one more attuned to our aging.
Looking back at living fifty years in this lovely dwelling place
calls forth a flood of passions.

It has been a home to three children
plunging into teenage years and growing towards adulthood.
Hundreds of neighborhood children were taught
to play from the vast piano repertoire by Sonia.
Many music lessons were enjoyed or not enjoyed
by our young ones as they beat the drums,
blew into a saxophone or
pulled a bow across violin strings.

We matured together
with tall graceful oaks, maples, and cedars
that cast shadows over our sloping rooftop.

Digging up our hoard of half a century,
we wonder. *Do we need this book, pen,
picture, clock, stocking, paperweight or file?
Must we discard that shirt, pair of shoes or tuxedo?*
Decisions do not come easily,
but they must be made – quickly.

We can never forget the chamber music evenings
with Sonia at the piano, thousands of hours spent listening
to treasures from our vast collection of shellac recordings,
78 rpms, 45 rpms, LPs and CDs.
Music with hearty dinners and vintage wine
brought many good friends to our table.

Is it time for a change?
Will we continue to enjoy life
or will we miss what we had?
In keeping with the flow of good living,
we will probably keep rolling on.

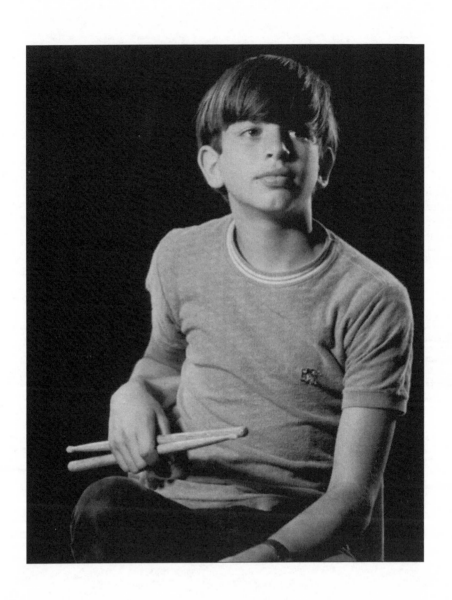

The Coming Out

Over 90 years of age, it now signals the end.
Still anchored firmly in my mouth,
it shows signs of aging, weariness and decay.
How many hunks of
meat, fish, celery has it ground down?
How many feasts has
it chewed for the swallowing?

The time has come to end its labor.
Soon it leaves a comfortable nook
in my gum to dangle in the air.
A long, workman-like life is ending.

It serviced me well but failed to outlive me.
Never, never will
a replacement show such loyalty,
faithfulness, such dogged commitment.

The Kiss

Sunday morning in a hospital is
no more exciting than a gray rainy day
in winter. In the elevator, a young woman
asks my daughter if I am her father.

Beth nods proudly, setting off a sigh
from our fellow passenger, "I lost mine last week;
he was sixty-one." With eyes glistening she asks my age.
When I reply that I am approaching ninety-one, she puts
her arms around me and says to Beth,
"How lucky, may I kiss him?"
A hug, a warm embrace and heartfelt kiss
pay tribute to her late father.
She bids us goodbye when we exit on floor eight.

I Am

New to living alone -
life is difficult, most strange.
Once I turned to my lover,
murmured, reflected, pontificated.
Now I whisper, joke, tease
with no one.
I confide, snicker no more.
Desolate.
The walls of loneliness are bare.

And yet,
beauty, fascination, and wonderment
cry to me.
They reach to me.

My writing, my music, my art.
They are the passageway
past the walls,
past the voices in shadows.
They lead to the door that opens -
the door my lover and I used to
call our own.

Secret To A Happy Union

Be open
Do not be stubborn
Relax
Do not have to win every argument
Avoid using sledgehammer
Respect your partner
Recognize that we are all different
Measure the consequence of each battle
Does winning build or destroy
Be kind
Be nice
Caress instead of clobber
Learn to live in a field of joy
Avoid narrow and stubborn thoughts
I did and it made life something to treasure
It lasted for 71 years
It left me with few regrets
I would do it again if she were still with us

Cambridge On The Charles

New to Cambridge at age ninety-four, I stare with wonder
at the vibrance of the old. Here, church spires
thrust into skies evenly, street after street.
Graceful slatted wooden houses of every shape
brave the heat and even winter's bitter blasts.

Parks and greenery grace almost every block.
Crowds of grim joggers pound city streets
with steely determination.
Droves of students stroll, joke, fill the streets between classes.
College buildings and dormitories are seen on almost
every winding street. Exotic eateries like Ethiopian cafes with
low tables and large trays of flat bread are all around.
Lectures, poetry readings in bookstores, concerts
ring out from corner to corner.

Ethnic culture reflecting the Far East, the Middle East, Africa
and Asia is as common as soap operas on afternoon TV.
The Red Sox, The Bruins, The Celtics, The Patriots dominate.

It is also the Mecca for medicine, higher education, scientific
research. Surely a good place to live, yet it has its quirks.
Homes are cold in winter.
Lighting in living rooms is low when entertaining guests.
This, my new home, is stimulating and dramatically different
from my Long Island abode of 50 years.

Peter The Great

Stormy outside, gloomy inside,
yet he glows within, full of sunshine.
Where does this gift from heaven come from and why?
Ours is a huge high-rise apartment with numbers of good
people and hundreds of children.
The lobby is quivering with
excitement because of Peter's presence
as concierge of Parkside Place.
He presides over the lives of residents of 250 apartments.
Residents entering, residents leaving
are met by cheerful hellos and warm goodbyes.
He greets all by first names with a broad smile.
No matter how young, he trades high fives with all the children.
He chats protectively with new residents,
always inquiring about welfare, problems and progress.
He opens doors, spreading his charm
to all he speaks to.
Reflections from his bald pate
reveal the path to the elevators.
Deliveries of meals, mail and
Amazon packages fill his day
as he directs this massive yet proud
village-like circle of residents.
He calls me King, I named him Prince of Peace.
Never a day goes by without his singing hellos
livening the lobby of 700 Huron.
He hails me as I step off the elevator
with a clear short cry "What do ya read?"

My move to Cambridge was worth it
if only for Peter.
Lonely elders drift to his desk to chat.
Residents wander past his desk on their way to the laundry
room. Parents and nannies stop to gossip
as they head for the children's playroom.
Clearly his being here adds charm and excitement
to the entrances and exits of this large and busy abode.

Songs Of Poetry Readings

Living in Cambridge, I am swimming
in a storm of poetry readings.
Clubs, studios, art centers and other
sites register the passionate vibrations
of poems singing through evening air.
Warm surges of appreciation sound the bells
of creative response.
An array of emotions swings in the minds of
listeners who sway silently to a poem being read.
Excitement rings out as each poet pours out his heart.

Riding Up - Riding Down

Entering my building elevator daily,
I move in gently as I look around,
careful not to bump into anyone.
I seek to meet the eyes of fellow riders
representing almost every continent on the planet
– they open up new worlds for me.
On one ride I speak in Arabic to two young women
wearing traditional head covering: "keef kon?" (how are you
both?)
On another, I chat
with a middle-aged couple from Russia and
tell them that my late wife was born there.
I add that every night for 71 years,
I murmured "ya tibya lublu" (I love you) at bedtime.
The stars of our lofty abode, the children,
light up the short ride with chatter and whining
while pulling at their mothers' clothes.
Students crowd into the car with backpacks stuffed with books.
Friendly folks meet my eyes and smile,
remembering previous elevator exchanges.
As riders leave, some sing out
greetings: "Have a good day," "Bonjour," "Sai chen."
The younger ones prance through the lobby
greeting those they know and trading high fives
with Peter the concierge.
All day long, like a miracle, the car methodically rises from the
ground floor, stopping to take in and release its passengers,
resumes its vertical trajectory to the top, then slides noiselessly
down to sea level.
Oh, how wonderful it is to traverse the globe
in this small and intimate chamber.

Green, Green, Green

My eyes are drowned in green – green trees,
green shrubbery and green spaces.
Where but the Boston area are there so many
green playgrounds, green ballfields and oh so
many green gardens sparked by spring
flowers in bloom?
Stretches of green grass surround homes
and driveways, filling the air with breezes -
pungent breath from the soil.
When strolling through greater Boston, I wallow
in green, green and green.

Bagel Bards

The whiff of toasted bagels
fills the air.
Poets of every breed sit
to breakfast while easy talk
dances to the drumbeat
of seasoned writers.
Some write prose,
others work at
poetry of the day.
Minus an agenda, talk is open
yet touched with humor.
What was the week like?
Who said what? When do we eat?
Newly published books are passed around
above warm cheese danishes and hot coffee.
Groups huddle in circles, the
more vocal holding forth.
The tradition so solid,
the buzzing sounds in meter.
Thus the Saturday morning for poets is to be treasured.
Long live the songs of Bagel Bard artists.

Joe's Bench

I pause and sit on Joe's Bench.
Matching my quiet mood,
Huron Ave. traffic slows down.
The sun's rays blanket the bench
with cozy warmth.
Often I greet joggers, bikers, and
strollers on the move.
Naming it for myself, I glory in the luxury of resting alone on it.
I listen to the gentle warm wind blowing through its curved
slats.
Few people in Cambridge know of its lone presence.
I am drawn to it when I seek an old friend.
Passersby stare at it but rarely sit on it.
I imagine seeing a halo gently embracing it when I approach.
I come to it on many a fair day.
I admire it! I adore it! I love Joe's Bench.

Made in the USA
Lexington, KY
21 August 2017